AF485303

LEADERSHIP MATTERS TO GOD

Published in the United states of America
ISBN: 9798787956733
Imprint: Independently published

1. Nonfiction > Business & Economics > Leadership
2. Nonfiction > Business & Economics > Organizational Behavior

TABLE OF CONTENTS

INTRODUCTION

Behold, I have given him for a witness to the people,
a leader and commander to the people.

Isaiah 55:4

What is leadership, really? What qualities make one person an effective or a mediocre leader? What qualities of leadership are effective for secular or Godly work? Can the same qualities be effective in both? Do the academic theories of leadership apply the same to the secular and Godly? Can the principles that are effective in secular leadership be applied to Godly leadership? How about the skills that a person brings as a leader? Do these skills apply in both secular and Godly leadership? How different and acceptable is the behavior in these two different worlds? Can one behave the same? Do you have to adapt in order to fit from one world to the other? It is said that an individual's personal attributes and distinctives are basic to who they are. So, is a particular personality a liability in one world and not another? Is having a particular management style an asset or liability? Is the objective the same for a project, work, mission, or program in the secular versus Godly work? What are the different results expected from secular versus Godly work?

The Secular World View

In the world of business higher education leadership is looked at through the eyes of academics. They seek to credential leaders through an accepted body of knowledge, based on the following:

- Credentials: candidates must be qualified based on their mastering of the body of knowledge within the curriculum before they are allowed to practice,
- Ethics: candidates must agree to a preconceived idea of what is the "public good" and a "code of ethics."

In stark contrast, the "real life" business community, corporation board room, and professional organizations all lean more toward client needs, professional knowledge, and practical experience. They are less concerned with leadership as a "gated & educated" profession which requires credentialing and licensing. They see the need for creativity, imagination, and experience for leadership to be effective and productive.[i] In general, this secular world view of effective leadership is based on a separate criterion.

- How does a leader provide client or customer satisfaction?
- How does a leader keep labor costs within an acceptable range?
- How does a leader handle losses, injuries, failures, deficiencies, or shortfalls in production?
- How does the leader focus on profit and loss, because that sets the stage for everything else?[ii]

An effective leader plays a crucial role which brings everything together. Without effective leadership, all other business resources are ineffective. Effective leaders must be aware of finances, employee issues, new industry developments, and how to create a more effective working environment.[iii]

The Kingdom View

A biblical view of leadership is not rooted in the secular world's concepts of success. It is not rooted in the secular world's view of money or power. Jesus spoke against these urges when expressing the importance of serving others, considering the poor, orphans, and true widows. Jesus' view of an effective Christian leader should be driven by:

- The love of God.
- Modesty and humility before God and others.
- Staying right with God.
- Making personal time to grow spiritually.
- Continually motivating others.
- Encouraging others in Christian love.
- Modeling and demonstrating biblical interests not secular ideologies.

Effective leaders in ministry set the example for others to follow. It's not about being perfect but leading. Effective leaders in ministry accept everyone, warts and all, seek forgiveness when they mess up, and admit their failures. Effective leaders in ministry earn the respect of others by being faithful and making a difference. Effective leaders in ministry serve others. Effective leadership in ministry is based on the quality of people's lives. It's not about money, it's not about achievements, it's not about numbers, it's about quality.[iv] So, what is the difference between the secular and Godly world views?

DEFINITION

So shall it not be among you:
Whosoever will be great among you,
Shall be your minister:
Whosoever of you will be the chief,
Shall be servant of all.

Mark 10:43-44

Secular World Definition

The secular world's definition of leadership understands it as a position or office. It is a persons' capacity to lead based on charisma, position, or function. This person must be able to guide, direct, and command others in order to accomplish a goal. This person is the one who is in charge or in command.[v] It is the leader of a group or organization. For the most part the position is contained for a specific time or identifiable status. It is the power or ability to lead other people.[vi] As Former first lady Rosalyn Carter is quoted as once having said:

> *"A leader takes people where they want to go. A great leader takes people where they don't necessarily want to go, but ought to be."*[vii]

Biblical Definition

The biblical definition of leadership includes a person of character, competence, and influence. This person has an impact not only on a church but on the larger community. Their aim is to achieve a God-honoring mission through the power of Christ.[viii] They meet people where they are and take them where Jesus wants them to go.[ix] Their intent is to act and speak in such a way to create a general understanding of a missional goal, set a high standard of ethics and professionalism all defined by God's Word.[x]

LEADERSHIP

BIBLE STUDY

Proverbs 14:28 (MSG)
> The mark of a good leader is loyal followers,
> Leadership is nothing without a following.

Proverbs 16:12 (MSG)
> Good leaders abhor wrongdoing of all kinds,
> Sound leadership has a moral foundation.

Proverbs 20:28 (MSG)
> Love and truth form a good leader,
> Sound leadership is founded on loving integrity.

Proverbs 21:1 (MSG)
> Good leadership is a channel of water controlled by God;
> He directs it to whatever ends He chooses.

Proverbs 25:4-5 (MSG)
> Remove impurities from the silver and the silversmith can craft a fine chalice,
> Remove the wicked from leadership and authority will be credible and God-honoring.

Proverbs 29:14 (MSG)
> Leadership gains authority and respect when the voiceless poor are treated fairly.

Please answer the following question:
- What are these verses saying about leadership?

LEADERSHIP

BOLAND

THEORIES OF LEADERSHIP

God saw that the wickedness of man
was great in the earth, and that every imagination
of the thoughts of his heart was only evil continually.

Genesis 6:5

How is a Christ-like leader supposed to lead effectively and purposely? Is that person the actual head of the church, or are they just a facilitator? Maybe they just organize and guide things along?

- Are they supposed to push people into compliance?
- Are they to pull others along grudgingly?
- Are they to ignore those who fail to follow willingly?

All of academics have their theories, why not religious? [xi] Should secular leadership theories apply toward the church? Business model leadership theories explain the how and why of business, such as:

- They describe professional leadership styles.

- They focus on the traits and behaviors people bring to management.

- They explain leadership capabilities and how other people adopt to that influence.

- They discuss the idea behind ethical and moral standards.

- They provide an insight into different organizational skills.

- They detail the different philosophies in dealing with employees.

The primary leadership theories are as follows. [xii]

The Transformational Theory

The transformational theory of leadership is also known by the term *relationship theory*. This theory indicates that a good leader is effective because of their ability to relate to people. As the result of these relationships, they can build an effective organization. These leadership skills motivate and inspire others by their enthusiasm and passion for their work or ministry. They set a standard or model for others to follow. They hold themselves accountable to that same standard they expect of others. Therefore, others follow willingly. It was in 1973 that a man named James Downton came up with this concept. Then in 1978, James Burns expanded on that model. Finally in 1985, Bernard Bass added success measures to the overall body of knowledge.[xiii] Leaders who are known for using the transformational form of leadership are Steve Jobs, Jeff Bezos, and President Obama.

Behavioral Theory

The behavioral theory of leadership looks at a person's environment, not their abilities. This theory considers a person's conditioning. This simply means a person will act or lead as a result of what is happening around them and respond to the behavior. The theory assumes the traits expressed by one leader can be multiplied by other leaders. Sometimes called the *style theory*. The assumption here is that leaders aren't born successful but can be created based on learned behavior. The behavioral theory looks at the actions of a leader and suggests that the best predictor of success is in their behavior. This theory centers on the action rather than the ability of the leader. Their behavior is observed and labeled. Some of the well-known labels include *task-oriented, people-oriented, country club, status-quo,* and *dictatorial,* etc. Beginning in 1913, Dr. John Watson, a U.S. psychologist published his findings in this area and is considered the father of behaviorism. His theory is in common practice by such businesses as IBM, Pepsi, Coca Cola, Nestle, and General Motors.[xiv]

Contingency Theory

The contingency theory of leadership is all about adapting to whatever one faces at the moment. This theory is sometimes called *situational theory.* It is also known by such titles as *Hershey and Blanchard's Situational Theory, Evans and House Path-Goal Theory,* and *Fiedler's Contingency Theory.* There is no certain type of leadership style here. Instead, the leader adapts based on the situation. They may respond to whatever is happening by taking command, coaching, persuading others, participating alongside, delegating authority, or doing whatever they think is necessary and appropriate. Situational leaders are defined by their flexibility. All these theories look at the success or failure of a leader based on how they adapted to any given situation. A leader's effectiveness is directly determined by the condition and context. Even though a leader's personality plays a part in their success, the most important factor is their ability to adjust to the context and circumstances. These theories all suggest that the best thing is to find the right kind of leader for a specific setting. Indra Nooyi, CEO of PepsiCo Global, Jack Stahl, former CEO at Revlon are identified as adherents to this theory. [xv]

The Great Man Theory

The great man theory of leadership, also called the *trait theory*, suggests that good leaders are born. Based on this theory, apparently, there are innate traits and skills that make certain leaders great. This stuff cannot be taught or learned. The theory believes that leaders are worthy and have been born to their position because of their special attributes. Therefore, excellent leaders are identified from birth, not developed. This was a popular concept in the 19th century (1800-1899). A leader in this category possesses intelligence, courage, confidence, intuition, and charm, etc. The theory was built on the mythology of the world's most famous leaders of past times such as Abraham Lincoln, Julius Caesar, Mahatma Gandhi, and Alexander the Great.[xvi]

The Management Theory

The management theory of leadership is also known as *the transactional theory*. This theory is based on a system of rewards and penalties. It views leadership effectiveness as results-based and hierarchical. The leader focuses on order and structure over creativity. The centerpiece of the theory is supervision, organization, and group performance. This theory is often observed in business. It is here where employees are rewarded for their success and punished when they fail. The idea is simple, people only do things for the reward, much like Pavlov's dogs. Their psychology doesn't allow human beings to do things out of goodness, but rather out of the promise of a reward. In 1947, Max Weber, a German sociologist, wrote out this leadership style and divided it into three categories: traditional, charismatic and rational-legal (bureaucratic). Hewlett-Packard is the best-known company using this theory. Individuals known to use this theory are Gen. Norman Schwarzkopf, Vince Lombardi, and Bill Gates.

The Participative Leadership Theory

The participative leadership is also known as *democratic leadership theory*. This theory is seen under another well-known theory, *French and Raven's Five Forms of Power*. This theory is not common in the corporate world. This theory involves employees in the direct decision-making of an organization. The leader is simply a facilitator. The leader has a meeting with employees, gets input, and then produces the best possible action. In this theory, everyone is very involved with decisions. This theory simply looks at the way the leader utilizes power and influence to get things accomplished. Such people who prescribe to this theory are Donald Trump, Jim Lentz, of Toyota Motor North America, Inc., Bob Diamond of England's Barclay's Bank, and James Parker of Southwest Airline.[xvii]

The Relationship Theory

The relationship theory of leadership focuses on the leader's interaction with others. The theory addresses mentoring, scheduling interaction, and visiting. This theory focuses on making an enjoyable work environment and fostering a positive work atmosphere. It is believed through some studies that this leadership behavior can be the most effective for many employees. Relationship-oriented managers often get better results. Businesses and corporations have depended on this theory since 2019. The pandemic has brought about a need for the greater use of conference calls, email, texting, video (zoom) conferences, social networking and other forms of interpersonal communication. These forms of communications have become crucial elements in building and maintaining relationships at all levels both in and out of the office, board room and among management. It was Professor Elton Mayo who first developed the Human Relations Approach to Management Theory He, Fritz Roethlisberger, T.N. Whitehead, and William Dickson, conducted their study on need and development of human relationships.[xviii]

BIBLE STUDY

1 John 4:1 (MSG)

My dear friends, don't believe everything you hear. Carefully weigh and examine what people tell you. Not everyone who talks about God comes from God. There are a lot of lying preachers loose in the world.

Ephesians 4:19-24 (MSG)

No going along with the crowd, the empty-headed, mindless crowd. They've refused for so long to deal with God that they've lost touch not only with God but with reality itself. They can't think straight anymore. Feeling no pain, they let themselves go in sexual obsession, addicted to every sort of perversion.

That's no life for you. You learned Christ! My assumption is that you have paid careful attention to him, been well instructed in the truth precisely as we have it in Jesus. Since then, we do not have the excuse of ignorance, everything—and I do mean everything connected with that old way of life must go. It's rotten through and through. Get rid of it! And then take on an entirely new way of life a God-fashioned life, a life renewed from the inside and working itself into your conduct as God accurately reproduces his character in you.

Please answer the following questions:
- Do secular world theories apply to kingdom ministries? If so, how?
- How should or how could kingdom leaders apply the secular world theories in their ministry?

LEADERSHIP

BOLAND

PRINCIPLES OF LEADERSHIP

Therefore, leaving behind the initial lessons
about the Messiah, let us go on to maturity,
not laying again the foundation of
turning from works that lead to death,
trusting God.

Hebrews 6:1 (CJB)

BIBLICAL PRINCIPLES[xix]

Love Matters

As believers we have been bestowed with the love of God. Therefore, we should put the biblical definition of love at the forefront of our life and work. Expressing love as a leader transforms the situation, condition, and organization. It cannot be emphasized enough how powerful, and influencing is the love of God when shown by leadership. Paul wrote about the transforming nature of love. He stated it builds up others faith and instills their hope. Jesus even told His disciples that other people will know them by their love.[xx]

Modesty Matters

The character of leadership which does not call attention to oneself, even though the talent, aptitude, or abilities are present and available. Scripture refers to opposite of this as prideful, arrogant, and haughty in spirit.[xxi] Scripture makes it a point to direct women to be modest.[xxii] Meaning to be extra careful not to over enhance themselves publicly. The men are not to be openly belligerent or aggressive with those they oppose but seek confrontation with them through prayer.[xxiii] Raising holy hands to God has more of an effect than physical altercations.[xxiv]

Time With God Matters

Biblically speaking, time alone in prayer is essential for every leader with a ministry purpose. Call it what you will a quiet time, time alone with God, meditation time, whatever. Real prayer time is essential and important for the leader of a ministry organization. They must manage it well. Not some period of time humming to yourself made to focus on one's navel! One cannot know God's Will without time alone with the master. One cannot visualize God's purpose for the future without time researching God's Word. Without purposeful time separated from the hustle and bustle of life's noise, one cannot focus on God's direction, blessing, and purpose in ministry.[xxv]

Motivating People Matters

Pastor Stephen Grunlan said it best, "Instead of misleading or exploiting people, good leaders motivate others."[xxvi] It is almost an art form in this day and age to correct, discipline, or warn someone in a way that doesn't hurt their feelings or damage their self-esteem.

The apostle Paul encouraged us to be peacemakers, encourage those who are unruly, and who are fearful. He encouraged us to support the weak, be patient with people who grate on our last nerve. He went on to say that we should avoid foolish and ignorant disputes, knowing those kind of discussions only generate conflict without any positive results. A true leader of God must not be quarrelsome but be gentle to all, able to teach, patient, and with all humbleness correct those who are in opposition to the Word of God. The way a leader does this is by the following:

- Understand the temperament of people,
- Respect the concerns of people,
- Identify the Spiritual Gifts of people,
- Use the Spiritual Gifts of people to the glory of God,
- Support the visions and dreams of those in ministry,
- Challenge, exhort, and redirect the flaws of people into ministry.[xxvii]

Discipline Matters

Motivating people is important and so is the principle of correcting them. Correcting others in the right way is critical to an effective functioning mission focused on honoring and glorifying God. Many passages in Scripture speak to this principle. We are called to encourage (exhort, reassure, inspire, help, or nurture) one another. We are to show appreciation (recognize, value, and acknowledge) and teach each other. To churches, Paul says, be at peace, do not be in conflict over trivial matters to the point you ruin your witness before a community. [xxviii]

Integrity Matters

Godly leaders practice and value honesty. They have a faithfulness to an inner moral code. They must know, seek out, understand, and follow God's Will. They prepare their heart before God. Before they answer, they pray. They commit their work to the Lord. Their thoughts are established before God. Leadership understands the plan, but God directs their steps.[xxix]

PRINCIPLES FROM MARK'S GOSPEL xxx

Faith-based organizations are called to stand out and be different than secular corporations, business, or industry. Leaders, who are believers, should also live differently in all workplaces, in accordance with Christian beliefs rather than worldly standards. The principles in the book of Mark help God honoring leaders make good decisions, lead effectively, and honor God in the workplace, marketplace, and ministry

A Good Reputation Matters

The reputation was so impactful and widespread that He drew crowds. These crowds followed Jesus because of His teaching and preaching. They came from miles around. They came from Galilee, Judea, Jerusalem, Idumean even beyond the Jordan, from Tyre and Sidon. The reputation principle directs us to conduct ourselves in such a way that others know who we are. They know we represent and point others to God. The Word of God surrounding the preaching and teaching of Jesus was so radically different from the culture of His day and continues to be impactful on the lives of people in our day because it is unlike other religions. Jesus did not die! He rose again! Leaders must not allow our reputation to stain His reputation.

They must perform their job with excellence. They must cultivate their reputation with honor. [xxxi]

Crisis Management Matters

In his book *A Father's Advice to His Son,* Rudyard Kipling wrote the best advice for leadership when in the middle of chaos:

> *"If you can keep your head when all about you*
> *Are losing theirs and blaming it on you,*
> *If you can trust yourself when all men doubt you,*
> *But make allowance for their doubting too!"*

Jesus' exemplified leadership under fire. His demeanor amid chaos was always cool, calm and without losing focus on the ministry. Yes, this is the Lord. OK, let's get that out of the way. However, the key principle is evident. Keep a clear mind, do not panic, do not allow distractions to take your focus away from the real issue, keep your attention on the crises at hand, be aware that there are those who are looking to you for guidance. The Scripture passages shows Jesus' handling a crisis as important. It indicates that we must trust the Lord and His sovereignty within the storms of life and gain peace and discernment from His Spirit's leadership. [xxxii]

Knowing When to Delegate Matters

As Jesus developed the ministry skills of the disciples, He delegated authority to them. This is the sign of true leadership. Not trying to accomplish all the tasks at hand by oneself. Jesus did not delegate out of inability, lack of time. The principle here that can be applied to leadership is one of trusting others to carry out different aspects of a project or mission which strengthens team building and gives others a sense of ownership in the process. Simply stated, we are not able to do everything on our own. There is a two-part lesson here: one, it lets others feel as if they are a creative part of the program; and two, it keeps balance in the life of the leadership.[xxxiii]

Conflict Management Matters

Even Jesus had to deal with petty disagreements. One was over who was the most important among His disciples. In settling this issue, Jesus set a high bar in dealing with inter agency conflicts. He addressed the situation quickly and directly. He began with a question rather than accusation. He reminded them of the importance of those in leadership having a servant's heart and putting others before themselves. The takeaways here are simple. Leaders should engage sooner rather than later, to avoid festering bitterness and discontent.

Leaders should seek to discover the root of the problem rather than assume or accuse anyone of misdeeds. Leaders should remind everyone of biblical principles and qualities embodied in Jesus Christ. [xxxiv]

Being Committed Matters

To the rich young man wanting to follow Jesus, He said "Go, sell all that you have and give to the poor, and you will have treasure in heaven; and come, follow me." That was a devastating blow to the ego of that man, but one that few of us will ever have to make in order to truly follow Jesus. However, He always asks for commitment from those that follow Him. As believers, we are asked to commit our entire selves to serving Him, including the work we do on a day-to-day basis whether that is at home, an office, assembly line, a professional, government, business, or school. The commitment is not just a Sunday thing. It is a Monday through Sunday thing.

In any organization, if the leadership is not committed, those around them will sense it, and it will affect the internal enthusiasm and effectiveness. Leadership helps build the character of any organization when they are passionate about what they are doing the focus is clear and the direction is known.[xxxv]

Faith Matters

Leadership must have an enormous amount of faith to accomplish God size projects. Faith is important, especially when others do not see the vision. progress, or the possible end. Mark chapter 11 challenges leaders to believe God even when they think the circumstances are overwhelmingly against them. Leadership is to have faith that moves mountains and know that God can do those big things for those who trust in Him. Surely, if the leadership doesn't believe God can accomplish, complete, or move obstacles out of the way neither will anyone else.[xxxvi]

BIBLE STUDY

John 8:32
> You shall know the truth, and the truth shall make you free.

Proverbs 3:3
> Let not mercy and truth forsake thee,
> Bind them about thy neck,
> Write them upon the table of thine heart.

Proverbs 8:7
> For my mouth shall speak truth,
> wickedness is an abomination to my lips.

Proverbs 12:17
> He that speaks truth seeks forth righteousness,
> But a false witness deceit.

Proverbs 12:19
> The lip of truth shall be established forever,
> But a lying tongue is but for a moment.

Proverbs 14:22
> Do they not err that devise evil?
> But mercy and truth shall be to them that devise good.

Proverbs 16:6
> By mercy and truth iniquity is purged and by the fear of the Lord men depart from evil.

Proverbs 20:28
> Mercy and truth preserve the king and his throne is validated by mercy.

Please answer the following questions:
- What principles do these verses focus?
- Why is truth so important to the Word of God?

LEADERSHIP

BOLAND

43

SKILLS AND LEADERSHIP

God's free gifts and his calling are irrevocable.
Romans 11:29 (CJB)

There are some basic skills that those wanting to go into leadership need to know. Anyone desiring to be an effective and productive leader should be a problem solver, decision maker, planner, manager, delegator, communicator, and organizer. These are basic and foundational from which to develop a more advanced understanding of management and leadership. Other skills that matter include:

Abilities and Talents Matter[xxxvii]

Abilities are the same as having know-how, experience, or competence. One's ability to do something determines whether or not they possess the means to actually get things done. For example: does one possess good communication skills? Do they think critically? Do they work well with others? Are they self-motivated? Can they think on their feet (flexibility)? How's their determination and persistence in any given situation? Do they cave in under pressure? Are they a quick learner when faced with a skill they do not know? Do they manage time well or are they always late for appointments? Talents are different too. These include such things as being innovative. Is the person adaptable? Do they have the power to persuade others? Do they have a good relationship with others, or are they a lone ranger?

Patience Matters

We have all heard the quote that patience is a virtue[xxxviii] but patience is crucial in leadership. The ability to not jump to conclusions, not get excited when facing critical issues, and losing your composure in front of others are necessary for a leader. One writer looked at patience in the following way. The world's greatest leaders are driven by the following: purpose, approachability, tolerance, independence, empathy, nurturing nature, confidence, and endurance. It's not a coincidence that these words make up the acronym patience.[xxxix] Leadership, it is said, means having purpose and sticking. Patience is essential for any kind of change to occur. Leaders must be open-minded. They must understand how valuable it is to be accessible by people they lead, and the community. They need to know the correlation between being open-minded and seeing long-term solutions. There needs to be an independent streak in them. However, they need to be honest, and straightforward. Although, it doesn't hurt to be somewhat defiant. They should lead with compassion and concern toward others. They have to know how to encourage and support others. The ability to stay cool collected and self-assured under pressure without being cocky and conceited goes a long way toward being successful. They shouldn't give up. They should understand that real and lasting success goes beyond short-term gains.[xl]

Empathy Matters

Leaders should have the ability to understand and share the feelings of another. Leaders need to understand the three types of empathy. Leaders may need to understand another person's thoughts and feelings in a situation but maintain an emotional distance. A leader may be consciously aware of another's feelings, meaning they simply know how the other person feels and what they might be thinking. Leaders need to be able to separate themselves from the emotional, meaning physically feeling what the other person is going through emotionally. The leader may be compassionate, meaning they may not understand a person's predicament and feel with them, but are moved to help, if needed.

Active Listening Matters

An effective leader must become an active listener by building trust and establishing rapport. Paraphrasing what is said helps demonstrate understanding. Using nonverbal cues which show understanding such as nodding, eye contact, and leaning forward indicate that one is involved in the conversation. Brief verbal affirmations also helps like "I see," "I know," "Sure," "Thank you," or "I understand."

Reliability Matters

A leader must be dependable, accurate, and dependable. This means someone who can be trusted in all circumstance, works hard, and does what is expected. A leader must be good for their word. They cannot be what some call two-faced, meaning to say one thing and not delivering. Leaders are seen as unreliable when they lie, show lack of transparency, breach confidentiality, or create an environment of uncertainty.

Dependability Matters

A leader must be punctual because being on time is more than just common courtesy. They must be able to communicate clearly and distinctly. They must be able to set deadlines and adhere to them because people are looking for clear direction and purpose from leadership. They must be able to take the initiative on important issues and matters and not let them hang out to dry waiting for others to deal with them. Leaders are expected to be detail-oriented because the organizations they lead will not succeed if others are expected to fill in the blanks. Leaders are the only ones that can build effective teams that work together.

Creativity Matters

God is the great creator of the universe. We have been created in His image. Therefore, every one of us is creative! Leaders are expected to be very creative individuals. Creativity is the ability of a person to generate new ideas, concepts, and visions. Leaders should be able to think outside the box of normality. They should be able to conceive something in a way that has not been done before.

Positivity Matters

Leaders are expected to be optimistic. When their company, organization, or mission is in trouble. When they are facing personal adversity. When they are in the middle of unexpected problems.

Timely Communication Matters

A leader is expected to get information to those who need it when it is appropriately needed and not delay or hold back. Timeliness refers to the expectation of material or information, its accessibility and availability. Timeliness is measured between when information is expected and available. Anything delayed is a problem of leadership.

Relationships Matter

Leaders must have strong, trusting, and authentic relationships with others. This includes both up and down the organizational food chain. They must realize that spending time building bonds with others makes more effective organizations. Leaders must understand that leadership is all about relationships. Leaders and managers with poor relationships will see performance, projects, and plans fail.[xli]

Flexibility Matters

Flexible leaders are those who can change their approach to management as they come. They revise plans as circumstances change while at the same time still achieving their intended goals.

Risk-Taking Matters

The risk-taker accepts the possibility of failure despite the potential. They encourage innovation, creativity, and change both in themselves and others. The pursuit of risk-taking is vital to a successful leader. Part of the quest to succeed in leadership is finding new or better ways of doing things or meeting the needs of others.[xlii]

Decisiveness Matters

This skill is important because it can be the difference between plans lacking direction and those focused on achieving objectives. A leader, who has the ability to make last minute decisions, seeks the appropriate information necessary to make good decisions. This leader does not quickly ignore or disregard information submitted at the final moment.

Integrity Matters

Integrity in leaders means to be honest, trustworthy, and reliable. They act and stand on their word. They accept their mistakes, as opposed to hiding them, blaming their team, or making excuses and go on.[xliii]

Problem Solving Matters

A leader must be able to identify the problem, then analyze the situation, and describe it clearly without bias. A leader must be able to look for the root causes of any situation if they intend to get past it. Just dealing with surface issues will not be clear enough or valuable. The leader then needs to develop all available alternate options with the intent of implementing a solution. After that, they must measure the results to see if other alternatives are warranted.

Ability to Teach and Mentor Matters

The Mentoring or discipleship process is a two-way street between the one leading and one learning. For it to be successful, both participants must work together.

- They must establish the goals for the mentee.
- They must establish the scope of responsibilities for each person, no assuming or speculation.
- They must understand time commitments and constraints.
- They must establish meeting times and places.
- They must establish how communications will take place.
- They must establish what is and is not confidential information.
- They must establish how information obtained during these times will be handled.
- They must establish what topics or issues are outside of bounds?
- They must establish what is the process for dealing with possible conflicts that may arise during their time together?
- They must establish how and when to end the relationship

Effective Mentoring is not a surprise. It is planned. The mentee needs a direct line of reporting to the mentor. The mentee needs to be held accountable for that which is shared. Over time an atmosphere of trust develops. The mentee feels comfortable sharing certain things and abilities. This relationship can be mutually satisfying. The mentor gets the satisfaction of watching someone grow. The mentee gains a feeling of value and receives direction. The amount of time spent in the relationship is in proportion with which both people are comfortable. This time committed must be flexible to both schedules. Reality states that at any time, the mentoring process can be stopped or delayed for a time or season. An effective relationship provides wise counsel, a comfortable environment to share and build trust. The mentoring process is about guidance and support rather than formal training.

Mentoring Relationships can go wrong for several reasons. One major reason would be a breach of trust by either party. Then there could be a conflict of values. This would be in a situation where either party could not compromise over some form of issue. Then there is the situation where one of the parties abandons the relationship. Most mentors go into the relationship sincerely intending to give their all, unfortunately, scheduling issues interfere creating excessive challenges leaving one or the other party feeling neglected and frustrated. Then there is the sense of manipulation, where one of the parties is using the relationship for personal gain or personal advantage. So, how do people in a mentoring relationship avoid such issues, by having the following:

- An up-front agreement between both parties.
- Venting both parties before getting involved.
- Mentors with appropriate training.
- Mentor volunteers with right skill sets.
- Matching mentors with the mentees or allowing the mentees to choose the mentors.
- Providing quick feedback from both parties about appraisals and progress.
- Beginning the process with an end date.

Everyone should be prepared to understand that mentoring will eventually end. Everyone should be prepared to understand that eventually mentees will turn into mentors for others.

BOLAND

BIBLE STUDY

Luke 4:16-22

He (Jesus) came to Nazareth, where He had been brought up. As was His custom, He went into the synagogue on the sabbath day, and stood up for to read. There was delivered unto Him the book of the prophet Esaias. And when He had opened the book, He found the place where it was written,

The Spirit of the Lord is upon me because He hath anointed me to preach the gospel to the poor; he hath sent me to heal the brokenhearted, to preach deliverance to the captives, and recovering of sight to the blind, to set at liberty them that are bruised. To preach the acceptable year of the Lord.

He closed the book, and He gave it again to the minister, and sat down. And the eyes of all of them that were in the synagogue were fastened on him. He began to say unto them, this day is this scripture fulfilled in your ears. All bare Him witness and wondered at the gracious words which proceeded out of His mouth. And they said, Is not this Joseph's son?

Mark 6:35-44

When the day was now far spent, His disciples came unto Him, and said, this is a desert place, and now the time is far passed send them away, that they may go into the country round about, and into the villages, and buy themselves bread: for they have nothing to eat. He answered and said unto them, you give them to eat. And they say unto Him, shall we go and buy two hundred pennyworths of bread, and give them to eat?   He saith unto them, how many loaves have you? go and see. And when they knew, they say, Five, and two fishes.

He commanded them to make all sit down by companies upon the green grass. They sat down in ranks, by hundreds, and by fifties.
When He had taken the five loaves and the two fishes, He looked up to heaven, and blessed, and break the loaves, and gave them to his disciples to set before them; and the two fishes divided he among them all. They did all eat and were filled. They took up twelve baskets full of the fragments, and of the fishes. They that did eat of the loaves were about five thousand men.

Matthew 4:23, 9:35, 11:1, 28:19
Jesus went about all Galilee, teaching in their synagogues, and preaching the gospel of the kingdom, and healing all manner of sickness and all manner of disease among the people.

Luke 24:30-33
And it came to pass, as He sat at meat with them, He took bread, and blessed it, and brake, and gave to them. Their eyes were opened, and they knew Him; and He vanished out of their sight. They said one to another, did not our heart burn within us, while He talked with us by the way, and while He opened to us the scriptures? They rose up the same hour, and returned to Jerusalem, and found the eleven gathered together, and them that were with them,

Please answer the following questions:

- What did the previous verses tell us about Jesus' skills?
- Why were the people of His home village surprised at His statement? What were they thinking?
- How do these skills apply to our lives today?

LEADERSHIP

BOLAND

BEHAVIOR AND LEADERSHIP

Now the works of the flesh are manifest, which are these;
adultery, fornication, uncleanness, lasciviousness, idolatry,
witchcraft, hatred, variance, emulations, wrath, strife,
seditions, heresies, envying, murders, drunkenness,
reveling, and such like...they which do such things
shall not inherit the kingdom of God.
The fruit of the Spirit is love, joy, peace, longsuffering,
gentleness, goodness, faith, meekness, temperance:
against such there is no law.

Galatians 5:19-23

SUCCESSFUL LEADERS MANAGE BY[xliv]

Ethics

A true leader is grounded in values and honesty. These are properties of successful people no matter what stage or level in life. Individuals who are committed to doing the right things for the right reasons will do it even under the most difficult or unpopular of circumstances. This gives emphasis to the idea of having and keeping consistently high professional standards.

Faith

A true leader is trustworthy. This is something easy to verbally toss around but not easy to prove. It is something that must be earned. This is earned over a series of consistently unambiguous and transparent actions. This is earned over time based on decision after decision thus proving trustworthiness.

Optimism

A true leader does not need a title to be influential. They encourage others. They help others to grow and achieve. They bring out the best in others. They look at people as individuals and treat them with respect.

Inspiration

A true leader inspires those around them. They have a vision that motivates people to follow. They express that vision with passion and energy. They back that vision with their beliefs and values. They cause others to get excited, engage, and uplifted at being a part of something bigger and better.

Confidence

A true leader is a decision maker. They are not afraid to make the hard decisions with authority and confidence. They make decisions by balancing emotion with reason, enlisting the opinions of others to ensure the move forward is well-informed, yet acting with authority. They are successful because they honestly communicate the underlying principle behind their decision for long-term success.

Creativity

A true leader is not afraid to give others the space to be creative in that individual's space. They create a culture which encourages the art of "possibility" thinking. They view every project or situation from outside the box. They are not intimidated by innovation and creativity from those who question, observe, experiment, and network with others.

Character

A true leader rewards achievement. No one likes to see their hard work and accomplish go unrecognized. They make it a habit of calling out others who make contributions to the organization, the project or whatever the mission or ministry purpose happens to be. This may be expressed through a physical reward or just a polite acknowledgement

Example[xlv]

A true leader walks the walk. They display the behavior they expect from others.

Collaboration

A true leader is transparent and thus builds the trust of those around them. Secrets will destroy any hope of trust. They are direct and honest. They realize that they are communicating all the time both in word and deed. They understand that a lack of information opens the door to negative assumptions that disrupt motivation and productivity. A true leader reveals only what is necessary, at the appropriate time they can reveal it. They quickly admit their mistakes when they are wrong and acknowledge limitations. They build a network of people who know more than they do about those knowledge areas they know little about.

Keeping Promises & Commitments

A true leader is trusted to keep their word no matter what. If it is out of your control, then say so.

Belief in Others

A true leader trust others until proven wrong. A true leader attempts to get the best out of others. A true leader attempts to trust others to lead. Trust is a two-way street. If you don't trust those around you, they won't trust you. As the sign on President Truman's desk once said:

The Buck Stops Here.

A true leader knows who is in charge and who takes the blame.[xlvi] In short, when something goes wrong, acknowledge the fact that the mistake was made under your leadership. Don't throw others under the bus.

Feedback

A true leader knows they are not perfect. All of us learn as we go. A true leader asks for feedback. What needs to be done better? How can we improve? What Do we need to change? How do we communicate better? When the feedback is provided, accepting it with grace and a thank you, even if it isn't easy!

Objectivity

A true leader learns that playing favorites exposes a double standard and loses trust quickly. Playing favorites destroys team building! A true leader treats everyone fairly

A true leader has the same expectations from everyone. Some leaders create environmental rules collectively which ensures that everyone agrees to uphold the same set of standards. A true leader sets clear expectations upfront, including clear roles and responsibilities. This ensures there are no surprises. A true leader doesn't get sucked into the gossip mill because gossip kills trust. True leaders set and follow a rule that if you are not part of the problem or a part of the solution you are not part of the conversation.

Listening

A true leader takes the time to get to know everyone they work with. A true leader asks questions, consistently, and then truly listens. A true leader learns much vital information that way by keeping quiet during discussions or meetings. There is value to letting others talking and explaining.

Consistency

A true leader knows that being unchanging in character, conduct, and temperament is essential to effective leadership. A true leader knows that calm in actions, behavior, mood, and expectations goes a long way to put an end to uncertainty, frustration, and distrust.

Inclusiveness

A true leader knows that selfish individualism doesn't win friends and creates enemies. A true leader shows others that they are important.

BOLAND

BIBLE STUDY

John 13:34-35

> A new commandment I give unto you, that ye love one another; as I have loved you, that ye also love one another. By this shall all men know that ye are my disciples, if ye have love one to another.

Luke 10:33-35

> But a certain Samaritan, as he journeyed, came where he was: and when he saw him, he had compassion on him, and went to him, and bound up his wounds, pouring in oil and wine, and set him on his own beast, and brought him to an inn, and took care of him. On the morrow when he departed, he took out two pence, and gave them to the host, and said unto him, take care of him; and whatsoever thou spend more, when I come again, I will repay thee.

Mark9:34-37

> But they held their peace: for by the way they had disputed among themselves, who should be the greatest. He sat down, and called the twelve, and saith unto them, If any man desire to be first, the same shall be last of all, and servant of all. He took a child and set him in the midst of them: and when he had taken him in his arms, he said unto them, whosoever shall receive one of such children in my name, receives me: and whosoever shall receive me, receives not me, but him that sent me.

Matthew 6:14-15

> For if ye forgive men their trespasses, your heavenly Father will also forgive you. But if ye forgive not men their trespasses, neither will your father forgive your trespasses.

Matthew 18:32-35

Then his lord, after that he had called him, said unto him, O thou wicked servant, I forgave thee all that debt, because thou desired me. Shouldn't not thou also have had compassion on thy fellow servant, even as I had pity on thee? His lord was wrath, and delivered him to the tormentors, till he should pay all that was due unto him. So, likewise shall my heavenly Father do also unto you, if ye from your hearts forgive not everyone his brother their trespasses.

Please answer the following questions:

- What behaviors do these verses point out?
- What do these verses encourage us to do?

LEADERSHIP

BOLAND

ATTRIBUTES AND LEADERSHIP

Keep a firm grasp on both your
character and your teaching.
Don't be diverted. Just keep at it...
1 Timothy 4:16a (MSG)

An attribute is a quality found in a person's character which is a deep-seated part of their being. [xlvii]

Character

An effective leader builds a reputation known for being trustworthy, respectful, responsible, fair, caring for others, and being a good citizen. An effective leader avoids being known for having emotional outburst, chronic sarcasm, being inflexible, being wishy-washy in decision making, being impatient, being a control freak, lacking empathy for others, or being closed-minded.[xlviii]

Visionary

No leader can be effective unless they have a vision for their work, mission, or project. Scripture says that,

Where there is no vision, the people perish.

An effective leader looks at what they are facing, considers the resources available, and sees the potential of achieving the goal. Without a vision the leader is unlikely to achieve anything significant either in the workplace or for the kingdom. An effective leader must be able to communicate that vision to others. An effective leader is able to articulate the vision in a way which inspires and encourages others.[xlix]

Focus

An effective leader must be dedicated to the task at hand. An effective leader reaches out to those who do not buy into or believe in what is being said or done. An effective leader continues to reach out to those who need to know and understand the meaning behind the work, and the purpose for it.[l] An effective leader has many responsibilities and duties. No one can avoid being distracted by the unrelated, irrelevant, unimportant, and superfluous. An effective leader stays on task knowing what is important and needs to be accomplished.[li]

Passion

An effective leader must be passionate about what they are doing. An effective leader must care deeply about their work, mission, or project and be committed to it. An effective leader's passion will encourage others to push on and succeed when obstacles arise.[lii]

Spirit-Led

An effective leader must believe in their cause. An effective leader must have a temperament and attitude to accomplish what they started out to do. In ministry, to be an effective leader one must remember that it is a partnership between them and God. No matter the type of leadership style, man may think they make their own plans, but God gives it direction.[liii] An effective leader never attempts to work alone or trust in their own power or abilities. An effective leader knows that they must seek to rely on others and God in all they do to stay focused and grounded.[liv]

Service

An effective leader must have the heart of a servant. Jesus was the foremost example of a servants attitude when He made the following statement,

I did not come to be served, but to serve.[lv]

An effective leader must remember that their role is to serve others. An effective leader runs contrary to the world's standards. The success of an effective leader is to watch those around them grow and succeed.

Courage

An effective leader must be fearless. An effective leader must stick to their beliefs when under attack, and to manage with confidence. An effective leader does not pander to the wishes of those around them. An effective leader demonstrates a willingness to step out in faith, have a reliance on God, and strength to do what is needed to accomplish the goal.[lvi]

Trustworthy

An effective leader must be unwavering in their beliefs. An effective leader trusts in God, relies on God's Word, believes in their abilities and in those around them.[lvii]

Organized

An effective leader must be prepared for all situations and conditions. An effective leader must expect the unexpected and be able to lead, manage, or minister in any situation. An effective leader understands sacrifice and planning. An effective leader understands that major crises will happen and prepares for that situation mentally, physically, and emotionally.[lviii]

Opportunistic

An effective leader must be resourceful in a good way and not in an unscrupulous way. An effective leader can navigate through difficult times as well as take advantage of new opportunities. An effective leader should take advantage of these unexpected opportunities and not just plan or stay stuck in the past. This means an effective leader is prepared and alert when those opportunities come along.

The Roman philosopher Seneca, stated the following about opportunity,

Luck is what happens when preparation meets opportunity.[lix]

The Apostle Peter put in a different way,

> *Be ready always to give an answer to every man*
> *that asks you a reason of the hope*
> *that is in you with meekness and fear.*[lx]

Sense of Community

Most secular leaders concern themselves with profits and material productivity. Biblical leaders concern themselves in terms of impacting relationships and people. Paul described his relationship to the Thessalonians as being warm-hearted toward them, being gratified to be a part of their lives, because they had become very dear to him. [lxi]

Reliability

Worldly leaders generally operate on their own terms, strength, and wisdom. They accomplish good and even noble things. Biblical leaders produce eternal results because it comes from a different source. Biblical leaders do not base their success upon individual terms, individual strength, or human wisdom. Their success cannot be accomplished by natural and human ways or by the limited skills of any leader. The biblical leaders rely on the very power of Christ!

Competence

An effective leader has a sense of when to delegate authority to others. An effective leader can manage projects and people. An effective leader knows how to communicate truth to others. These are unique distinctives all effective leaders must have for them to be successful. In this sense, outward competence is related to inward character.[lxii]

BIBLE STUDY

Matthew 9:36

But when he saw the multitudes, he was moved with compassion on them, because they fainted, and were scattered abroad, as sheep having no shepherd.

Mark 10:45

For even the Son of man came not to be ministered unto, but to minister, and to give his life a ransom for many.

Luke 23:34

Then said Jesus, Father, forgive them; for they know not what they do

Luke 6:36

Be merciful, even as your Father is merciful.

John 15:13

Greater love has no one than this, that someone lay down his life for his friends.

Please answer the following questions?

- What did the previous verses tell us about the attributes of Christ?
- How do these attributes apply to our lives today?

LEADERSHIP

BOLAND

STYLES
OF LEADERSHIP

Listen carefully to my wisdom;
take to heart what I can teach you.
You'll treasure its sweetness deep within;
you'll give it bold expression in your speech.
To make sure your foundation is trust in God,
I'm laying it all out right now just for you.
I'm giving you thirty sterling principles
tested guidelines to live by.
Believe me these are truths that work,
and will keep you accountable
to those who sent you.
Proverbs 22:17-29 (MSG)

1. Don't walk on the poor just because they're poor. [lxiii]

2. Don't use your position to crush the weak,
    a. God will come to their defense,
    b. What you took, he'll take from you and give back to them.[lxiv]

3. Don't hang out with angry people.

4. Don't keep company with hotheads,
    a. Bad temper is contagious don't get infected.

5. Don't gamble on the pot of gold at the end of the rainbow,
    a. Don't pawn your house against a lucky chance,
    b. The time will come when you have to pay up,
    c. You'll be left with nothing but the shirt on your back.[lxv]

6. Don't stealthily move back the boundary lines staked out long ago by your ancestors.[lxvi]

7. Observe people who are good at their work,
    a. Skilled workers are always in demand and admired,
    b. They don't take a backseat to anyone.[lxvii]

LEADERSHIP STYLES

The leadership style a person takes on when managing others is simple. Each style is broken down into classifications of how a person behaves while leading others. In 1939, psychologist Kurt Lewin determined that there were three basic styles of leadership: authoritarian (autocratic), participative (democratic), and delegative (laissez-faire). Since that time, several other categories have been recognized.[lxviii]

Coach

This style of leadership recognizes strengths and weaknesses of those around them. This leader helps people set goals and provides feedback. This leader focuses on bringing out the best in others by guiding them through objectives and obstacles. This leadership style is very much opposite to autocrats, who are focused on top-down decision making.

Visionary

This style of leadership manages, inspires, and builds the confidence of those around them. This leadership ensures the vision becomes reality by stating clear goals, outlining a premeditated plan for achieving those goals. This leader equips and empowers everyone involved in the decision-making process.

Servant

This style of leadership focuses on helping those around them feel fulfilled in whatever they are doing. A servant leader attempts to enrich the lives of individuals and create a just and caring world.[lxix]

Autocratic

This leadership style makes decisions with little input or creativity from anyone else. They manage with total decision-making power and absolute control.

Laissez-faire

This style of leadership is sometimes considered lazy because they delegate tasks and provide little supervision. In fact, the laissez-faire leaders are known to have trust and reliance on those around them. They don't micromanage. They don't get too involved in the assignments of others. They don't give too much instruction or guidance. They give guidance and take responsibility where needed. They allow subordinates and others to lead, while they direct.

Democratic

This style of leadership is sometimes criticized for being wishy-washy because they consider the opinions of others before making any decisions. A democratic leader has a style of participatory leadership. They allow those they work alongside participate in the decision-making process.

Pacesetter

This style of leadership is criticized for being too pushy because they set high standards and focus on performance. They are obsessed with getting things done better and faster. They set the bar high for themselves and others. They never ask of others what they wouldn't do themselves.

Those working alongside this individual are expected to perform in the same manner. This style of leadership can be good to reach short-term results. They are detrimental for the long-term project.

Bureaucratic

This style of leadership follows a strict hierarchy and expects team members to follow procedure. Their leadership style is based on a fixed official duty based on a hierarchy of authority. They establish a fixed system of rules for management and decision-making.

Transformational

This style of leadership approaches their management in such a manner that causes change in individuals and work environment. They create valuable and positive change in those they work alongside, with the end goal of developing coworkers into leaders. They motivate others with their moral conduct and character. They connect with others through their sense of identity and self-assurance to the mission purpose. They exude a sense of collective identity and loyalty for the organization, mission, and work. They are a role model for others that inspires them and challenges them to take greater ownership for their work.

They seem to have an uncanny understanding of the strengths and weaknesses of others as they align others with tasks that optimize their performance.

Transactional

This style of leadership values order and structure. They functional well in a military operation, managing large corporations, or leading international projects that require rules and regulations to complete objectives on time or move people and supplies in an organized way. Transactional leaders are not a good fit for places where creativity and innovative ideas are valued.

JESUS LEADERSHIP STYLE

Servanthood

When the disciples quarreled about their position, Jesus refused to dignify their discussion. He preferred to demonstrate servanthood. [lxx]

Loving

Jesus demonstrated to them that the way people would be convinced that they were his followers would be their obvious love for one another.[lxxi]

Practical

Jesus lived what he taught. He was able to challenge his accusers, knowing they fabricated falsehoods. Therefore, Pilate testified to the excellence of Jesus leadership when he remarked,

I find no fault in his man.[lxxii]

In view of this, true leaders should be what they teach. They must match words with deeds! Jesus never caved to temptation, strayed from the ideals of His service, or used His power to dominate others. The gentile leaders, on the other hand, lorded their power over those they ruled. Jesus did not!

Humility

Jesus was such a humble leader that his disciples were amazed to see him wash their feet. Jesus severely rebuked the Pharisees for wearing ornate clothing, taking the places of honor, being greeted submissively, and having people call them rabbi. Jesus did not use His authority for his own personal ambition. [lxxiii]

BOLAND

BIBLE STUDY

Mark 9:33-37

He came to Capernaum: and being in the house He asked them, what was it that you disputed among yourselves by the way? They held their peace: for by the way they had disputed among themselves, who should be the greatest. He sat down, and called the twelve, and saith unto them, If any man desire to be first, the same shall be last of all, and servant of all. He took a child and set him in the midst of them: and when He had taken him in his arms, He said unto them, whosoever shall receive one of such children in My name, receives Me: and whosoever shall receive Me, receives not Me, but Him that sent Me.

Mark 10:35-45; Matthew 20:25-28

James and John, the sons of Zebedee, come unto him, saying, Master, we would that thou shouldest do for us whatsoever we shall desire. He said unto them, what would you that I should do for you? They said unto him, Grant unto us that we may sit, one on thy right hand, and the other on thy left hand, in thy glory. Jesus said unto them, you know not what you ask:

- Can you drink of the cup that I drink of?
- Be baptized with the baptism that I am baptized with?

They said unto him, We can. And Jesus said unto them, You shall indeed drink of the cup that I drink of; and with the baptism that I am baptized withal shall you be baptized. But to sit on my right hand

and on my left hand is not mine to give; but it shall be given to them for whom it is prepared. When the ten heard it, they began to be much displeased with James and John. Jesus called them to Him, and saith unto them, You know that they which are accounted to rule over the Gentiles exercise lordship over them; and their great one's exercise authority upon them. So, shall it not be among you: but whosoever will be great among you, shall be your minister and whosoever of you will be the chief, shall be servant of all. For even the Son of man came not to be ministered unto, but to minister, and to give his life a ransom for many.

Please answer the following questions:

- What is Jesus idea of true leadership?
- What is the secular world view of leadership?

LEADERSHIP

BOLAND

RESULTS OF LEADERSHIP

You can develop a healthy, robust community
that lives right with God and
enjoy its results only if you do the hard work
of getting along with each other,
treating each other with dignity
and honor.

James 3:18 (MSG)

EFFECTIVE LEADERSHIP
vs.
INEFFECTIVE LEADERSHIP

An effective leader is also a balanced leader. An effective leader gets to know the people they work with enough to understand what motivates each person. An effective leader knows how to balance management and the workforce. It is by developing relationships among the workplace that the right conditions are created to bring about an effective and successful business strategy.

An effective leader has results-driven employees who want to know how they fit into the overall plan. These people need to know what happens if plan A fails. These people need a leader who is decisive and clear headed in decision making.

An effective leader, who has relationship-driven employees must be kind, interact with them on a regular basis and keep them in the loop. The leader must demonstrate care and concern for each one personally. They must feel a sense of ownership of the project, program, and work schedule. The key here is that this group is feelings based. They want to think that the leader considers them a friend and cares about them. Their thinking is I will work hard for friend and family.[lxxiv]

When an organization has an effective leader, everyone knows it and that generates a unique work environment. With effective leadership and work environment that isn't forced, and is natural, everything flows smoothly. The focus is on the mission, the vision, or the goals. All participants are fully involved and free to give input into improving the process. Everyone feels ownership of what is going on. Everyone believes in the decision-making process and senses that it is based on honesty, and integrity. The result of good leadership is high morale, strong support, and long-term success.[lxxv]

Signs of an Effective Leader

- An effective leader cares about others.[lxxvi]
- An effective leader is willing to lead by example and service.[lxxvii]
- An effective leader focuses on people more than success.[lxxviii]
- An effective leader has an impact toward excellence.[lxxix]
- An effective leader mentors others and develops future leaders.[lxxx]
- An effective leader is a positive force.[lxxxi]
- An effective leader promotes honesty and morality.[lxxxii]

An ineffective leader, on the other hand, has the opposite chilling effect. The signs of an ineffective leader are obvious.

Signs of an Ineffective Leader

- Lacks communication skills.[lxxxiii]
- Sets impossible standards.
- Difficult to be around.[lxxxiv]
- Emotionally draining to those around them.
- Frustrates the feelings of others.[lxxxv]
- Both uninspiring and unmotivating.
- Does not encourage others.
- Gives no clear direction and is inconsistent.[lxxxvi]
- Unreliable with communication style.[lxxxvii]
- Has no idea how to fit in to the scheme of things.[lxxxviii]
- Has no sense of ownership in what is going on.

Ineffective leaders can be demoralizing throughout the entire organization. The work environment becomes a meaningless term where leaders claim it exists while employees shake their heads in frustration. The problem is directly linked back to their ineffectiveness. As a result, the rumor mill runs wild. It is within this environment that employees or participants use tactics to gain an advantage over others. Participants are uncertain as to the goals and objectives for success. Whatever decisions being made are not based on integrity, talent, or logic.

Decisions are based on who can talk the biggest talk and deemed to be the least threatening to the power base. The environment becomes toxic. The result of bad leadership is low morale, minimal work effort, and a decreased ability to have any sustainable success.[lxxxix]

What Makes an Ineffective Leader?

- They do not care about people.
- They create an environment where no one wants to improve and do their best.
- They often make a majority of people around them to feel unimportant.
- They often only care about the results, numbers, and their personal success.
- They create a toxic work environment which leads to poor self-esteem of others.[xc]
- They take credit for the work of others.[xci]
- They show aggressive behavior toward other people.[xcii]
- They have that trickledown effect on those around them through their bad example, poor work ethics, and negativity.[xciii]
- They cause those around them to become disengaged and unresponsive to requests. [xciv]

BOLAND

BIBLE STUDY

Proverbs 16:10 (MSG)
> A good leader motivates, doesn't mislead,
> doesn't exploit.

Proverbs 16:12 (MSG)
> Good leaders abhor wrongdoing of all kinds;
> sound leadership has a moral foundation.

Proverbs 16:13 (MSG)
> Good leaders cultivate honest speech;
> they love advisors who tell them the truth.

Proverbs 19:12 (MSG)
> Mean-tempered leaders are like mad dogs;
> the good-natured are like fresh morning dew.

Proverbs 20:2 (MSG)
> Quick-tempered leaders are like mad dogs,
> cross them and they bite your head off.

Proverbs 25:4-5 (MSG)
> Remove impurities from the silver and the
> silversmith can craft a fine chalice;
> Remove the wicked from leadership and authority
> will be credible and God-honoring.

Proverbs 28:2 (MSG)
> When the country is in chaos, everybody has a plan
> to fix it, but it takes a leader of real understanding to
> straighten things out.

BOLAND

Please answer the following questions:
- What qualifies a Godly leader?
- What makes an effective leader?
- What makes an ineffective leader?

LEADERSHIP

BOLAND

CONCLUSION

So, what is leadership, really? Kingdom leadership is quite different from that of the secular world. What makes it different is what the bible describes as one person's influence upon another. What motivates that influence? Is it the type of outcome the influencer is seeking? Is it the power source that guides and sustain both the influencer and those being influenced? Is it biblically based kingdom leadership?[xcv]

What qualities make one person an effective versus mediocre leader? Very simple, mediocre leaders are not clear in the direction, orders, or vision. They do not listen to their staff, advisors, or constituents. They micromanage staff because they are dismissive of any idea but their own. They value familiar over new and creative. They lack compassion for others. They are not interested in mentoring future leadership. They seek only positive input. They have poor communication skills. They only delegate in order to assign blame. Effective leadership is quite the opposite. [xcvi]

What qualities of leadership are effective for the secular world but aren't transferable to kingdom work? Can any of these qualities be effective in both? The answer is a resounding no, because they do not have the same end goal in mind. One fact of leadership is that it doesn't exist apart from the leader. Biblical leadership focuses on Jesus Christ as a role model. A kingdom leader recognizes the fact that unless they change on the inside, any external changes will not make a difference. Secular world leadership dismiss the need for internal change. They design programs with predetermined solutions aimed at external behaviors.

Leadership is not normally transferable between the secular world and the kingdom work, because they do not have the same goal in mind.

Kingdom leaders must understand their calling. Kingdom leaders must concern themselves with multiple questions about their leadership. Why are they leading? What purpose do they serve as leader? Who are they leading? They must first answer the why, before the what and who! They must establish their purpose for leading. Their purpose is not what they do or even how they do it. Purpose is the "Why" behind what is done. Purpose is what differentiates Kingdom leadership from the rest of the culture. They must understand that character counts! The results of kingdom leadership are not about "whatever works" but building inner character that establishes moral qualities and distinguishes believers from the secular world. These qualities include things such as honesty, courage, integrity, humility, perseverance, and decisiveness. Kingdom leaders must be competent. Their skills are not something they use at "work" to provide profit for an employer.

Their skills and talents are not something one can put on or take off. Kingdom leadership ability cannot be disconnected from one's character. It is a piece of the inner person. Kingdom leadership is a demonstration of God's calling before the world.[xcvii]

Do academic theories of leadership apply to both the secular world and kingdom work? Well, they haven't so far. However, it should not come as any surprise that is what is happening! This is due to the structurization and institutionalization of denominational church leadership. Academic leadership theories are making inroads. For many years, leadership scholars have largely ignored the topic of religious leadership.[xcviii] What are called the pioneering studies were introduced in 1944 & 1968.[xcix] It was not until after 2000 that a plethora of studies were brought forth.[c] Then there came the production of several academic journals devoted to the study of Christian leadership. The *Journal for Biblical Perspectives in Leadership* (JBPL) and *the Journal for Applied Christian Leadership* both address scholarly ideals of ministerial leadership.

How about the skills that a person brings as a church leader? Do these skills apply in both worlds? Here is where there is a problem within the church. The Bible rarely talks about a "stand-alone leader." It addresses a plurality in leadership.

There is scriptural evidence that New Testament churches were to be led by leadership teams made up of bishops, elders, and deacons.[ci] In the New Testament these terms are used to designate offices which are appointed based on the individuals' skills, gifts, and character.[cii] The very idea that the New Testament used the terms to talk about a single leader ruling or governing the church alone is not there.[ciii] However, one would not know this by the widespread accepted use of the positions by some current denominations, independent, and community churches.

The Bible rarely talks about a "stand-alone leader."
New Testament churches were to be led
by leadership teams made up of
bishops, elders, and deacons.

If a person's attributes and distinctives are basic to who they are and sets them apart from other people, are any of these a liability in the secular world versus kingdom work? Secular thinking has always been a drawback to theological thinking. Consider the fact that "Wall Street" influences the church today. Unfortunately, to some it is welcomed and encouraged. While others see it as unbiblical and causing chaos. The sacred to secular divide debate is not new, of course.

It occurred between the Greek philosophers and first century Christians. It spilled out over Aristotelian physics, then with the Ptolemaic model of the universe, and even with the Galileo discoveries. To name just a few. How a person is educated and trained becomes a part of them. If they leave the secular, certainly they will bring into the sacred this knowledge. They will find it hard because as scripture states that no man can serve two masters for either he will hate the one and love the other; or else he will hold to the one and despise the other.[civ]

Is having a particular management style an asset or liability? A simple answer is yes. Most accepted management styles found in the secular world has no place in God's Work. For example, secular leadership has no issues with using threats to achieve managerial ends. Kingdom leaders are warned not to use this style of management.[cv] This creates seriously negative conditions, such as: employees, volunteers, or members are left without a sense of ownership. Employees, volunteers, or members begin to view their work as lacking value or being over valued by the leadership. It is also not surprising to see secular leaders dominate their work environments in order to achieve projected goals. Kingdom leaders are again warned not to use this style of management either.[cvi] This is insulting, disrespectful, and comes across as micromanagement.[cvii]

LEADERSHIP

Is the objective of a project, work, mission, or program all that matters for the secular world versus kingdom work? For the most part the central objective of the secular leadership is profit and loss, not people's feelings, personal lives, or spiritual conditions. The central objective of kingdom leadership is the process of helping people accomplish God's purposes. This was obvious in Jesus Christ's relationship with His disciples. How He related to them as people, and how He taught and encouraged them to teach others so the gospel would reproduce. [cviii]

What are the results expected from the secular world versus kingdom work? The question should really be: What results should we see from a kingdom leader? The motivating factor among any kingdom leader must be to cultivate a disciple-making community. This community must reproduce reproducing believers who bear witness to the Lordship of Jesus Christ. This must be a call to action in all that we think, say, or do. Kingdom leaders must shape the community of faith through true one-to-one discipleship. Kingdom leaders must be positive, confident, encouraging, and affirming how they deal with individuals. Kingdom leaders must not advance purposes or activities through negative, discouraging, or disapproving activities.

Kingdom leaders must not be influenced by secular world standards of size, numbers, or performances. Kingdom leaders must not cave to the secular world ideology of emotion, repetition, or inclusion being first, foremost, and fundamentally. Kingdom leaders must strictly adhere to the scriptures in its original form, as closely to its original language and understand its original historical context. Kingdom leaders should not cave to the demands of the current culture.

BIBLIOGRAPHY

INTRODUCTION

[i] *How Business Schools Lost Their Way*, by Warren Bennis and James O'Toole
Harvard Business Review, (May 2005)

[ii] https://www.businessandleadership.com/

[iii] https://www.ceoinstitute.com/leadership-training/the-importance-of-business-leadership

[iv] The Markers of Strong Biblical Leadership, By Dan Reiland, Outreach Magazine, (2021)
https://outreachmagazine.com/features/leadership/67709-the-markers-of-strong-biblical-leadership.html

[v] The American Heritage Dictionary, 3rd Edition, Houghton-Mifflin, Boston (1993)

[vi] "Leadership." Merriam-Webster.com Dictionary, Merriam-Webster, https://www.merriam-webster.com/dictionary/leadership. Accessed 6 Aug. 2021.

[vii] Lewis, Jone Johnson. "Rosalynn Carter Quotes." ThoughtCo, Aug. 26, 2020, thoughtco.com/rosalynn-carter-quotes-3530170.

DEFINITIONS

[viii] Power to Lead: Five Essentials for the Practice of Biblical Leadership, by Mike Ayer, RBK Publishing Group (2018)

[ix] *What is Biblical Leadership? by Todd Engstrom,* (2013)
http://toddengstrom.com/2013/11/11/what-is-biblical-leadership/

[x] Interview with John Piper, Founder & Teacher, desiringGod.org
https://www.desiringgod.org/interviews/what-is-leadership

THEORIES

[xi] *Leadership theories and styles.* Western Governors University (2021)
https://www.wgu.edu/blog/leadership-theories-styles2004.html#close

[xii] *6 Leadership Theories for Career Growth* By: Indeed Editorial Team (2021)
https://www.indeed.com/career-advice/career-development/leadership-styles-and-theories

[xiii] A guide to transformational leadership, .Western Governors University (2020)　　　　https://www.wgu.edu/blog/guide-transformational-leadership2008.html#close

xiv UKEssays. (November 2018). Behavioral Theory With Reference To Coca Cola Company Business Essay. Retrieved from https://www.ukessays.com/essays/business/behavioral-theory-with-reference-to-coca-cola-company-business-essay.php?vref=1

xv BusinessEssay. (2021, September 26). Contingency Theory and Global Leadership. Retrieved from https://business-essay.com/contingency-theory-and-global-leadership/

xvi The Great Man Theory of Leadership, By Kendra Cherry

Updated on September 17, 2020, Medically reviewed by Amy Morin, LCSW https://www.verywellmind.com/the-great-man-theory-of-leadership-2795311

xvii https://futureofworking.com/5-famous-participative-leaders/

xviii *Human Relations Theory of Management – Explained,* What is the human relations theory of management? Written by Jason Gordon, Updated at April 8th, 2022 https://thebusinessprofessor.com/en_US/management-leadership-organizational-behavior/human-relations-theory-of-management

PRINCIPLES

xix *What Is Christian Leadership?* 8 Principles, 2021 Campbellsville University. https://online.campbellsville.edu/ministry/christian-leadership-principles/

xx 1 John 4:8; Romans 5:5; John 13:35; 1 Corinthians 13:1-3; 1 John 2:15, 3:1-23

xxi Proverbs 16:18, Isaiah 16:6, Zephaniah 3:11

xxii 1 Timothy 2:9, 1 Peter 3:3-4

xxiii James 1:19

xxiv Proverbs 16:18-19; 1 Timothy 2:9-10

xxv Luke 22:41-44; Matthew 14:23; Mark 6:46; Luke 9:18; John 6:14-16; John 17

xxvi *Cultural Anthropology,* by Stephen A. Grunlan , Marvin K. Mayers, Zondervan Academic; Second edition (1988)

xxvii Nehemiah 2:17, Hebrews 10:24-25; 1 Thessalonians 5:13-14; 2 Timothy 2:23-26.

xxviii Hebrews 10:24-25; 1 Thessalonians 5:13; 1 Timothy 3:7

xxix Proverbs 16:1, 3, 9, 13

xxx https://faithsearchpartners.com/6-executive-leadership-principles-from-

the-gospel-of-mark-2/
[xxxi] Mark 3:7-8 (ESV)
[xxxii] Mark 4:35-39 (ESV)
[xxxiii] Mark 6:7 (ESV)
[xxxiv] Mark 9:33-36 (ESV)
[xxxv] Mark 10:21 (ESV)
[xxxvi] Mark 11:22-24 (ESV)

SKILLS

[xxxvii] *Leadership Skills: Definitions and Examples* By: Indeed Editorial Team, (2021) https://www.indeed.com/career-advice/resumes-cover-letters/leadership-skills

[xxxviii] stated as "suffraunce is a soverayn vertue", *The Vision of Piers Plowman*, by William Langland (c 1370) http://bibleornot.org/origin-of-patience-is-a-virtue/

[xxxix] Eich, Ritch (2017) "*Commentary: On Patience in Leadership*, "The Journal of Values-Based Leadership: Vol. 10 : Iss. 1 , Article 8.
Available at: http://dx.doi.org/10.22543/0733.101.1178
Available at: http://scholar.valpo.edu/jvbl/vol10/iss1/8

[xl] Eich, Ritch (2017) "Commentary: *On Patience in Leadership*, "The Journal of Values-Based Leadership: Vol. 10 : Iss. 1 , Article 8.
Available at: http://dx.doi.org/10.22543/0733.101.1178
Available at: http://scholar.valpo.edu/jvbl/vol10/iss1/8

[xli] cityandguildsgroup.com
https://www.oxford-group.com/insights/why-leadership-about-relationships

[xlii] *How Taking Risks Evokes Leadership Success, by* Megan Tull, Contributor (2017) Huffington Post
https://www.huffpost.com/entry/how-taking-risks-evokes-l_b_10843744

[xliii] https://www.sigmaassessmentsystems.com/integrity-in-leaders/

BEHAVIORS

[xliv] *7 of the Most Effective Leadership Behaviors*, Notre Dame, Mendoza College of Business Online (2019)
https://www.notredameonline.com/resources/leadership-and-management/7-leadership-behaviors-that-build-success/

[xlv] *12 Leadership Behaviors That Build Team Trust, by* Ekaterina Walter, Forbes Magazine, (2015)

https://www.forbes.com/sites/ekaterinawalter/2015/12/01/12-leadership-behaviors-that-build-team-trust/?sh=73e8aac47221

[xlvi] Sign on President Truman's desk in his White House office, made in the Federal Reformatory at El Reno, Oklahoma. United States Marshal for the Western District of Missouri Fred A. Canfil, had it made and delivered on October 2, 1945.

ATTRIBUTES

[xlvii] https://faithlifeministries.net/being-a-biblical-leader/

[xlviii] Proverbs 4:23

[xlix] Proverbs 29:18

[l] Matthew 28:19

[li] Daniel 3:13-18

[lii] Proverbs 16:3

[liii] Proverbs 3:6, 16:9; Isaiah 61:8

[liv] John 15:5

[lv] Matthew 20:28

[lvi] 1 Corinthians 13:16

[lvii] Proverbs 3:5

[lviii] 2 Timothy 4:2

[lix] *Luck Is What Happens When Preparation Meets Opportunity,* by Jill Griffin Forbes online Magazine, (2019) https://www.forbes.com/sites/jillgriffin/2019/04/09/luck-is-what-happens-when-preparation-meets-opportunity/?sh=4560456669c4

[lx] 1 Peter 3:15

[lxi] 1 Thessalonians 2:8.

[lxii] Exodus 18:13–27; Nehemiah 4:13–23; Colossians 1:28–29

[lxiii] Proverbs 14:31

[lxiv] Proverbs 22:22-23-22-23

[lxv] Proverbs 13:11, 1 Timothy 6:10, Hebrews 13:5, Matthew 6:24, Ecclesiastes 5:10

[lxvi] Deuteronomy 19:14, Proverbs 22:28

[lxvii] Exodus 35:35, Isaiah 41:6-18, 1 Chronicles 28:21

STYLES

[lxviii] Journal of Change Management 17 (2), 2017, DOI: 10.1080/14697017.2017.1299371., *Introduction: Kurt Lewin: 70 Years*

On, by Bernard Burnesa and David Bargalb

[lxix] *THE LEADERSHIP STYLE OF JESUS CHRIST IN THE NEW TESTAMENT AND ITS*
RELEVANCE FOR AFRICA, by MICHEAL T. KATOLA1 & BERNARD GECHIKO NYABWARI2 1Senior Lecturer and Former Chairman of Philosophy & Religious Studies, Kenyatta University, Kenya 2Lecturer Department of Philosophy & Religious Studies, Kenyatta University, Kenya

[lxx] Luke 9:46-48

[lxxi] John 13:34-35

[lxxii] Luke 23:4, 14; John 19:4,6

[lxxiii] John 13:34-35, Mathew 23:5-7, John 19:6, Mathew 4:1-11, Mark 1:12-13, Luke 4:1-3, Mark 10:42-44

[lxxiv] *Leadership style: Balancing results vs relationships, by Pete Hinojosa | Director, Sales Leadership Development Houston, Texas, Insperity*
https://www.insperity.com/blog/leadership-styles/

[lxxv] *Five Combination Traits of an Effective Leader (2019)*
https://www.forbes.com/sites/ellevate/2019/10/10/five-combination-traits-of-an-effective-leader/?sh=5e113054ad2b

[lxxvi] Proverbs 22:11

[lxxvii] Proverbs 20:26

[lxxviii] Provers 29:12

[lxxix] Proverbs 20:8-9, 28

[lxxx] Proverbs 16:10

[lxxxi] Proverbs 14:28

[lxxxii] Proverbs 16:12-13

[lxxxiii] Proverbs 17:7

[lxxxiv] Proverbs 16:14

[lxxxv] Proverbs 16:14

[lxxxvi] *6 Effects of Good Leadership on Employees* BY Dragan Sutevski,
https://www.entrepreneurshipinabox.com/13305/6-effects-good-leadership-employees/

[lxxxvii] Proverbs 17:7

[lxxxviii] Proverbs 28:16

[lxxxix] *The Impact of Good Versus Bad Leaders on a Company* By Seena Mortazavi
Association for Talent Development , (2013)
https://www.td.org/atd-blog/mentoring-diverse-distributed-and-digital-workers, entrepreneurship in a box

[xc] Proverbs 28:2

[xci] Proverbs 16:10

[xcii] Proverbs 19:12

[xciii] Proverbs 31:4-5

[xciv] *The impact of great and terrible leaders*, by Jacob Morgan, LEADERSHIP NOW (2020) https://www.leadershipnow.com/leadingblog/2020/01/the_impact_of_gre at_and_terrib.html

CONCLUSION

[xcv] *5 Distinctives of Biblical Leadership*, by Mike Ayers, Gospel-Centered Resources from Midwestern Seminary, (2016) https://ftc.co/resource-library/blog-entries/5-distinctives-of-biblical-leadership/

[xcvi] *15 Traits of a Terrible Leader*, By YEC, Success Magazine, (2017) https://www.success.com/15-traits-of-a-terrible-leader/

[xcvii] *How different is biblical leadership from worldly leadership?* (2021) Lead Like Jesus. https://www.leadlikejesus.com/qa/how-different-biblical-leadership-worldly-leadership

[xcviii] *"Prophet or loss? Reassessing Max Weber's theory of religious leadership,"* in D. N. Freedman & M. J. McClymond, The rivers of paradise: Moses, Buddha, Confucius, Jesus and Muhammad as religious founders (pp. 613-658). Grand Rapids: Wm. B. Eerdmans Publishing Company

[xcix] *Sociology of Religion* Chicago: University of Chicago Press. *Economy and society: An outline of interpretative sociology* (G. Roth & C. Wittich, eds., Vols. 3). New York: Bedminster Press.

[c] *Freedman, D. N., & McClymond, M. J. (2001). The rivers of paradise: Moses, Buddha, Confucius, Jesus and Muhammad as religious founders. Grand Rapids, MI: Wm. B. Eerdmans.*

Whittington, J. L., Pitts, T. M., Kageler, W. V., & Goodwin, V. L. (2005). Legacy leadership: The leadership wisdom of the Apostle Paul. The Leadership Quarterly, 16, 749-770.

Bekker, C. J. (2008a). The turn to spirituality and downshifting. In F. Gandolfi & H. Cherrier (Eds.), Downshifting: A theoretical and practical approach to living a simple life (pp.102-121). ICFAI Press: Hyderabad. Bekker, C. J. (2008b). Leading with your head bowed down: Lesson in leadership humility from St. Benedict of Nursia. Inner Resources for Leaders, 1(3), 1-10.

[ci] 1 Timothy, Titus, Philippians

cii Titus 1:5–9; 1 Tim. 3:1–7
ciii 1 Timothy 5:17; Titus 1:5; James 5:14
civ Matthew 6:24
cv Ephesians 6:9
cvi 1 Peter 5:3
cvii *What's Best Next Study Guide: How the Gospel Transforms the Way You Get Things Done* by Matt Perman, Zondervan, (2019)
cviii Matthew 28:19-20